Snoozefest

The Surprising Science of Sleep

Written by Tanya Lloyd Kyi
Illustrated by Valéry Goulet

Kids Can Press

ACKNOWLEDGMENTS

Thank you to Dr. Laura McLean, sleep medicine specialist, for reviewing the manuscript and providing wise suggestions. Thank you also to Kathleen Keenan, Jennifer Stokes, Amy Tompkins, Olga Kidisevic, Kathy Vanderlinden, Doeun Kwon and Barb Kelly for bringing the book to fruition!

Published in Canada and the U.S. by Kids Can Press Ltd.
25 Dockside Drive, Toronto, ON M5A 0B5

Kids Can Press is a Corus Entertainment Inc. company
www.kidscanpress.com

The artwork in this book was rendered digitally.
The text is set in Picadilly.

Edited by Jennifer Stokes and Kathleen Keenan
Designed by Barb Kelly

Printed and bound in Shenzhen, China, in 03/2021 by C & C Offset

CM 21 0 9 8 7 6 5 4 3 2 1

Library and Archives Canada Cataloguing in Publication

Title: Snoozefest : the surprising science of sleep / written by Tanya Lloyd Kyi ;
illustrated by Valéry Goulet.
Names: Kyi, Tanya Lloyd, 1973 – author. | Goulet, Valéry, 1978– illustrator.
Identifiers: Canadiana 20200389750 | ISBN 9781525301490 (hardcover)
Subjects: LCSH: Sleep —Juvenile literature. | LCSH: Sleep — Physiological aspects — Juvenile literature.
Classification: LCC QP425 .K95 2021 | DDC j612.8/21 — dc23

Kids Can Press gratefully acknowledges that the land on which our office is located is the traditional territory of many nations, including the Mississaugas of the Credit, the Anishnabeg, the Chippewa, the Haudenosaunee and the Wendat peoples, and is now home to many diverse First Nations, Inuit and Métis peoples.

We thank the Government of Ontario, through Ontario Creates; the Ontario Arts Council; the Canada Council for the Arts; and the Government of Canada for supporting our publishing activity.

Contents

Introduction

Get out of bed, lazybones!
The early bird catches the worm.
Rise and shine!

Have you ever heard these words? Do you desperately press your pillow over your head when your mom whips open your curtains in the morning?

"I need five more minutes," you mumble.

Well, here's an eye-opener: you might be right!

Our society doesn't always value sleep. But scientists know that shut-eye is vital to health, intelligence, memory, coordination, emotional stability, body weight, creativity, happiness and more. It turns out a good night's sleep might help us remember more information than a late-night study session, and a catnap might improve coordination more than a karate class.

How?

As we drift off to dreamland, dozens of cells and systems set to work. Antibodies zoom around like the late-night cleaning crews at Disneyland. Nerve cells turn our new experiences into long-term memories. Our blood pressure drops, our stress responses decrease and our growth hormones increase. All of this happens without our conscious knowledge.

The science of sleep is relatively new: until the 1950s, scientists thought of night as a dormant phase, a waste of time. Now they know it's the opposite. They also know most of us aren't getting enough rest. The average teen needs a little more than nine hours of sleep for all those systems to finish their work; in North America, the average teen actually gets more like seven hours.

Finding time to snooze has become more complicated in recent years. Friends who text late at night, TV shows that get your adrenaline racing, schools with early morning classes — these are all things scientists say are harmful to your health. Tweens and teens are especially vulnerable. It's tricky to balance modern life with the body's preprogrammed sleep needs.

In these pages, you'll find stories about the strange history of snooze science. You'll read about breakthroughs that rocked the world's cradles, and you'll uncover the surprising activities that happen in your body and brain once you drift off to dreamland. Do you love late nights and lazy mornings? You'll soon learn why.

Prepare to discover the learning, memory and healing systems that your conscious mind has never met.

Chapter 1

The ABCs of Zzzzz

Looking for a place to conduct sleep research? How about a dark, drippy cave, with a selection of centipedes for neighbors? No? What about the far reaches of the Arctic Circle, where the sun barely shines? Or a concrete bunker, deep underground?

Sleep scientists are a dedicated bunch. They've gone where practically no one has gone before. They've studied drowsy cockroaches, translucent tadpoles and time-telling bees. They've experimented on themselves and their own children. And sometimes, they've discovered amazing things by accident.

The history of sleep research is almost as strange and interesting as sleep itself.

A Psychic Mystery

In the middle of a military exercise, Hans Berger's horse reared, throwing the young German officer head over heels onto the road — and directly into the path of an oncoming artillery wagon. Hans looked up to see a huge wheel looming above his head. He was sure he was about to die.

The driver of the wagon stopped just in time, and — *whew!* — Hans survived with his skull intact.

Later that day, he received a telegram from his father. Hans's sister had been overwhelmed by the feeling something terrible was about to happen to Hans. She'd begged her father to check on him.

Coincidence or telepathy? Hans believed his mind had sent out a frantic call for help and his sister's mind had received that call, even though she was far away.

The idea sent Hans on a lifelong quest. He became a doctor in 1897, then a professor in 1906. He spent years trying to figure out how the human brain works and whether it could telepathically communicate. First, he tried to measure differences in blood flow. Then he looked for variations in the temperature of the brain. Finally, he turned to electricity. Other scientists had already shown that the brains of rabbits and monkeys produce energy. By implanting tiny silver wires beneath patients' scalps, Hans began to see the same electric currents in humans.

He spent decades refining his methods and equipment. By 1924, he could attach silver electrodes to the front and back of a patient's scalp, then track the tiny electrical signals on a rolling drum of paper.

Many of his fellow scientists thought he was weird. His test subjects looked like strange robots, all wired up, and Hans couldn't explain how the electrical signals were produced. He simply knew they were important ... somehow.

Hans never proved the existence of telepathy. But he did invent a machine that would change sleep science forever. With his wires and electrodes, he created the first electroencephalogram, better known as the EEG.

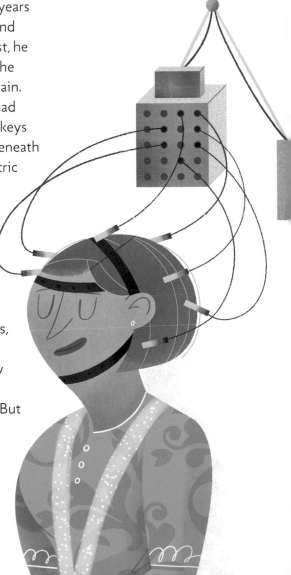

Waves and Wiggles

Picture your classroom. Now, picture every student at every desk quickly scribbling notes and passing them to the students on all sides — front, back and diagonally.

That's basically what's happening inside your brain right now. Your neurons, or nerve cells, are constantly communicating. They send their "notes" via tiny chemical and electrical pulses. Each note-passing connection is called a synapse. In a baby's brain, there are 100 billion neurons and 50 trillion synapses. That's more than the number of stars in our galaxy!

If that note-passing were happening in your classroom, you'd probably hear a buzz of activity and excitement. In your brain, the connections between cells create a buzz of electricity. It's enough electricity for electrodes — small pieces of metal — to detect. Electrodes can't measure the pulses of each neuron; those are too small. But they can read the overall patterns.

During an EEG, a technician attaches electrodes to a person's scalp. Those electrodes hook to wires, which in turn connect to a needle resting on a rolling drum of paper. As the electrodes read electrical currents, the needle moves up and down on the moving paper, creating a pattern of wavy lines. (Today, the lines appear on a computer screen rather than paper.)

When a person is awake, the lines appear as many little squiggles, showing that lots of neurons are firing in all directions. That's the equivalent of your whole class note-passing at once.

When a person is deeply asleep, the neurons fire more regularly, in a more coordinated pattern. The wavy lines made by the EEG machine are slower and larger. It's as if your friends have settled down and started to work on their assignments. Now they're all acting in a more synchronized way.

Each neuron has three parts:

- a cell body, which contains the nucleus
- a long, branching axon, which sends messages
- many branching dendrites, which receive messages

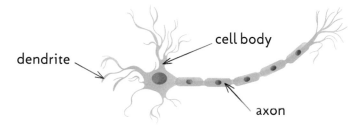

dendrite

cell body

axon

The Cavemen

In 1938, two researchers had a conversation that must have gone something like this:

Nathaniel: Hey, let's move into a cave!
Bruce: Yes! Let's choose one with total darkness.
Nathaniel: A place where sunlight can't reach us.
Bruce: Let's stay for a month. Maybe more.

Nathaniel Kleitman was a Russian-American professor at the University of Chicago. He was one of the world's first dedicated sleep researchers, with his very own sleep laboratory. Bruce Richardson was a twenty-year-old student focusing on sleep research. And somehow, they both thought moving underground was a great idea.

Nathaniel and Bruce wanted to know if the human body was designed for a twenty-four-hour day or if it could be reprogrammed. By living deep in Kentucky's Mammoth Cave, where temperatures didn't vary and sunlight didn't penetrate, they thought they might be able to change their own wake-sleep cycles. So they tried switching to a twenty-eight-hour day. They would sleep for nine hours, work for ten, rest for nine and repeat.

Babies have more nerve-cell connections than adults. As we age, we strengthen the connections we need most and get rid of the ones we don't use. So if you're a track star, you'll have lots of connections to control muscle movement and speed. If you never practice your spelling, you might not keep as many connections to help you spell M-I-S-S-I-S-S-I-P-P-I.

9

The experiment had a few downsides. Centipedes, for example! The researchers had to put the legs of their beds into buckets of water to keep creepy-crawlies out of their sheets.

But did the experiment work? Could sleep cycles be reprogrammed? Well, Bruce adjusted to the new schedule a bit better than Nathaniel. But both men found that no matter how they arranged their time, their body temperatures continued to rise during the day and drop at night. Even without a sunset to cue them, they grew sleepy in the evenings. Apparently, the human body followed a twenty-four-hour clock, and that clock wasn't easily altered.

Bruce and Nathaniel had discovered something called the circadian rhythm. That's a combination of the Latin words *circa*, meaning "about," and *diēm*, meaning "day."

Whether or not you're living deep in a cave, your body keeps you on a sleep-wake cycle that lasts about a day. Some people veer from that cycle, but it takes longer than a month and usually happens in the complete absence of light. Blind people, for example, are more likely to experience a change in their circadian rhythms.

For the rest of us, it's rise and shine each morning, zonk out each night.

Concrete Findings

Years after Bruce and Nathaniel experimented with sleep in Mammoth Cave, two other scientists built their own kind of cavern. Rütger Wever and Jürgen Aschoff created a concrete bunker far underground near Andechs, Germany. Between 1964 and 1989, they conducted 418 studies on 447 men and women (as well as on birds and monkeys). Much of what scientists now understand about circadian rhythms came from those underground studies.

Tick-Tock Talk

Your heart can tell time. So can the outer layer of your eye and the inside of your liver. In fact, there are cells all over your body tick-tocking along to their own internal clocks. Their ability to stay on schedule is genetic. Because humans have risen with the sun and slept in the dark for millions of years, we're now preprogrammed for a cycle about twenty-four hours long.

The "boss" of the body's time-telling system is an area in the base of the brain called the suprachiasmatic nucleus. Even scientists think that's a ridiculously long name, so they call it the SCN.

There are about 20 000 neurons inside your SCN. They use their genetic programming to keep them on track. They also receive time-telling messages from light-sensitive cells in the retinas of your eyes. (That's why going outside in the sunshine helps people recover more quickly from jet lag.)

From its deep-brain control center, the SCN sends instructions to many other parts of your body.

- It raises your body temperature in the day and drops it at night.

- It tells the pineal gland deep in your brain to produce hormones that help you feel more awake or more sleepy.

- It works with neighboring brain regions to help you feel hungry during the day instead of late at night.

The SCN might have other jobs, too. Scientists still don't know exactly how it works or all the ways it communicates with the rest of the body.

In 1910, a Swiss psychiatrist named Auguste Forel was eating toast and marmalade on the balcony of his vacation retreat. Bees began to buzz around him. The next morning, the bees returned, just in time for breakfast. They seemed to remember what time the marmalade had appeared. Even after Auguste began eating indoors, the bees showed up on schedule for a few more days. Apparently bees, like humans, have their own internal clocks.

Family Travels

Sleep scientist Nathaniel Kleitman thought about sleep *all* the time. At his house, bedtime wasn't ordinary. He was constantly tracking his daughters' sleep patterns. He even set up cameras in their cribs to see how often they moved.

After serving as her father's guinea pig for years, Hortense Kleitman became a scientist, too. She studied sociology at the University of Michigan. And in 1951, she collaborated with her dad on a research project.

Nathaniel and Hortense traveled to the small Norwegian City of Tromsø, deep within the Arctic Circle. It's so far north, the sun never sets during the summer. The researchers had heard that in July and August, the people of Tromsø hardly ever went to bed. According to other Norwegians, folks in Tromsø ate so much fish and got so little sleep, they were all strange.

So Nathaniel and Hortense hired an interpreter and interviewed one hundred local residents. It turned out that these northern residents went to bed at about the same time as southern Norwegians — adults tucked themselves in at about 10:30 p.m. in the winter and between 11:00 p.m. and midnight in the summer. People slept for an average of 8.5 hours in the winter and 7.5 hours in the summer.

So even in the far reaches of the Arctic, where the amount of light varies dramatically, sleep schedules were only slightly different than those elsewhere in the world. And the residents of Tromsø weren't so strange after all!

Lucky Breaks

Clock cells aren't the only thing keeping our sleep on track. Hormones play a big role, too.

One of the most important is called melatonin. It's produced by the pineal gland, a tiny pinecone-shaped spot near the center of the brain. As it grows dark outside, the pineal gland gets to work, pumping out melatonin and sending it through the bloodstream to receptors in our brains and organs. It's the biological equivalent of your dad peeking through your bedroom door and calling, "Time for bed!"

So how did scientists discover how melatonin works? Completely by accident.

- In 1917, Carey Pratt McCord and Floyd Pierpont Allen were studying tadpole growth. They added a cow's crushed pineal gland to a tank of tadpole water and noticed that the little swimmers turned partly see-through. *Huh*, thought Carey and Floyd. *That's weird.* No one investigated further for fifty years.

- In 1958, a Yale University researcher named Aaron B. Lerner was researching skin diseases. He discovered that the pineal gland produces a hormone, and he named that hormone melatonin.

- In 1961, biologist Virginia Fiske at Wellesley College noticed that light affected rats' pineal glands. The glands seemed to produce more hormones after dark.

- In 1968, an American scientist named Julius Axelrod finally put all these discoveries together.

Nocturnal animals such as hedgehogs and skunks produce melatonin at night, too. In those animals, the hormone seems to signal active time rather than sleep time.

Julius figured out that melatonin is a form of the hormone serotonin (sometimes called the "happiness hormone"). It works as a signal from the pineal gland to other parts of the body. When that signal is picked up by receptors in a tadpole's skin, it causes color changes. But when it's detected by human brains, it does something completely different: it signals sleepiness. Julius won the Nobel Prize in Physiology or Medicine in 1970. (He probably should have thanked the tadpoles.)

Today, some people take melatonin supplements to help them sleep or to deal with jet lag. It seems to help people with chronic insomnia — those who have trouble sleeping many nights of the week. Scientists are still studying its usefulness and safety in other areas. You'll read more about melatonin in Chapter 5.

Subspecies: Night Owl

Phase delay.

It sounds like a *Star Wars*–style weapon malfunction. But researchers use the term to describe teen sleep patterns. Studies in Canada, the United States, Poland, Belgium, Australia, Finland and Brazil have all shown the same thing: most teens go to bed later than the rest of the world.

Part of this is probably because teens have busy lives. They're juggling homework, part-time jobs, sports teams and social events. In South Korea, college-bound young people take extra classes on weeknights, sometimes until midnight.

But does busyness explain all of teens' night-owl tendencies?

Apparently not. Even those who don't study late into the evenings, even those who don't get sucked into reality TV, *still* stay awake longer than young children and adults.

It's called "phase delay" because the sleepy phase of the circadian rhythm seems to be delayed until long after dark. Researchers have found the same delay in adolescent monkeys, degu (little Chilean rodents), rats and laboratory mice. None of those creatures are texting late at night. So what's going on?

There must be a biological explanation.

Professor Mary Carskadon at Brown University might have the answer. Every summer, she invites fourteen teens to her sleep laboratory. The campers spend their days and nights in an underground dorm, playing various games. The entire time, they're hooked to brain monitors. At various points during the day and night, they give saliva samples so Mary and her researchers can test their hormone levels.

Mary's looking for clues to explain why teens sleep differently than adults. Here are some of her findings:

- Teens need the same amount of sleep each day as younger kids: about 9.25 hours.
- Teens produce melatonin later in the evening than children and adults.
- Even when they've been awake a long time, teens don't get sleepy as quickly as younger kids.

It's as if teens are living in a different time zone. Something unusual is obviously happening inside their brains.

You might remember the health talks given by your school nurse. The ones about all the changes of puberty? It seems that some of those hormone and body changes in teens have side effects. They mess with sleep. And while Mary and her fellow scientists don't yet know exactly how or why the side effects happen, they *do* know that teen sleep-ins aren't a sign of laziness. They're a biological need.

But try telling that to the principal! (In Chapter 5, you can read more about Mary and her suggestions for high-school principals.)

To-Do List
- [ ] Math homework
- [ ] Saxophone practice
- [ ] Science fair project
- [ ] Soccer game
- [ ] Youth group
- [ ] Watch Netflix
- [ ] Text friends
- [x] Sleep

Eye Spy

Alfred Lee Loomis was an American lawyer and an investment banker and an inventor and a sleep science pioneer — and maybe a bit of a genius, too.

In 1918, he created a machine to measure the speed of bullets. He helped develop radar. He contributed to the early stages of atomic bomb research. Then, in the 1930s, he turned his attention to slumber.

Using an EEG machine, Alfred learned that people sleep in repeating patterns. He tracked the differences between brain waves in light sleep and deep sleep, and discovered that people cycle through these stages again and again during the night.

Twenty years later, sleep researcher Nathaniel Kleitman and an assistant named Eugene Aserinsky added another interesting finding. They were trying to figure out if people's eyeballs moved while they were sleeping. Did their eyelids flutter? Did they stop blinking all at once or slowly?

They started by watching babies, but Eugene couldn't see a definite difference between baby blinks and quivering eyelids. When he tried to watch older kids and adults, it was too dark to properly study their eyes. The usual brain-wave tracking machine, the EEG, couldn't tell him if his subjects' eyes were moving.

Finally, by combining the EEG with a small home-movie camera, Eugene found his evidence. He managed to show that during sleep, people's eyes sometimes moved back and forth, at the same time as their brain waves became more active. When he woke his subjects during this time, they reported having intense dreams. Eugene and his supervisor, Nathaniel, had discovered a new stage of sleep.

On Stage

Another of Nathaniel's students, a researcher named William C. Dement, was equally interested in dream research. Eventually, he suggested that people experience five sleep stages. The first two are light sleep, the next two are deeper sleep and the fifth is the dream phase. In the 1980s, scientists began combining the two deep-sleep stages into a single category, leaving them with four stages. Here's the list that's most commonly used today:

Stage 1: Your body's relaxed, your attention fades and you begin drifting away. Your brain waves are moving at half their normal speed. But you're only lightly asleep — if someone slams a door nearby, you'll jerk to wakefulness again and start the process over.

Stage 2: Your heart rate slows and your temperature drops. Your slow brain waves are now mixed with waves that look like the letter K on the EEG machine, as well as faster waves called "sleep spindles." (More on these in Chapter 2.)

Stage 3 (previously stages 3 and 4): Now you're in the deepest of sleeps, when the body heals and repairs itself. If your mom wants to wake you up, she'll have to call loudly or maybe shake your shoulder before your eyelids will flutter. Much of this stage is made up of high-power, slow brain-wave activity called delta waves. Remember when all the kids in the classroom were passing notes and then they settled down to work on one activity? This is your settled and focused phase of sleep.

REM: This is the rapid-eye-movement stage that Nathaniel and Eugene discovered. Your brain is almost as active as it is when you're awake. Your heart rate rises, you breathe more quickly and you burn more energy. During this stage, you have your longest and most vivid dreams.

The sleep scientists weren't the most creative name choosers. They called this newly discovered stage REM for "rapid eye movement." The other stages, they called NREM. You guessed it: "non-rapid eye movement."

Most people cycle through all sleep stages about once every ninety minutes during the night.

Common Sleep Sense

Alexander Borbély was a Swiss professor with unruly hair. It stuck up in all directions as if Alex hadn't slept in days.

But maybe he was just thinking hard.

To Alex, the circadian rhythms that Nathaniel and Bruce had experienced in Mammoth Cave didn't explain everything about our sleep cycles. If sleep was based entirely on a twenty-four-hour cycle, why would a late night make us sleepier the next day? Why would an afternoon nap allow us to stay up later that evening? The circadian rhythm by itself didn't make sense.

In 1982, Alex proposed that we have two sleep systems. The first is the circadian rhythm. The second is what Alex called "sleep pressure."

The human body likes stable conditions. It likes to stay in balance. Scientists call this homeostasis. If you're too hot, you'll automatically start to sweat as your body tries to cool down. If you forget to drink during soccer practice, you'll get thirsty. And if you stay up too late at a sleepover, you'll want to nap the next day. It doesn't matter that your circadian rhythm says, "Daylight! Time to be active!" You're sleepy because your body wants to regain its balance.

You don't need to stay up all night to feel this craving, either. Even after a busy day, you'll experience sleep pressure in the evening. Then, as soon as you get a good night's rest, the pressure disappears.

With his simple idea of sleep pressure, Alex had suggested something that would influence all the researchers who came after him: a two-process model. He said circadian rhythms and sleep pressure work together. Sometimes (post-sleepover, for example) they even work against one another.

Today, Alex's two-process model allows researchers to predict when people will be sleepiest and when they'll be most alert. It's used by hospital administrators to plan shift schedules, by doctors to help treat jet lag and even by the National Aeronautics and Space Administration (NASA) to schedule activities in space.

NASA astronauts want to make wise sleep choices, just like the rest of us. Read on to discover how scheduling a good sleep can actually make our brains work better.

HEY!

Chapter 2

Snoring Ourselves Smarter

In 1921, German professor Otto Loewi fell asleep while fretting about a research problem. Then, in the middle of the night, he had the answer — the perfect experiment to prove his theory! He grabbed a pen and quickly scribbled down his ideas.

There was only one problem: in the morning, Otto couldn't remember his ideas, and he couldn't read his own notes. Luckily, he had the same dream on the following night. The second time, he wrote more carefully.

While he slept, Otto had figured out exactly how nerve cells use chemical messages to communicate. He later won the Nobel Prize for his discovery.

But why was Otto's brain whirling away in his dreams?

Well, it seems that we all think while we snooze. And scientists are discovering more and more ways that intelligence, memory and creativity all depend on a good night's rest.

The Synapse Sweep

According to these stories, Otto wasn't the first person to make a discovery in his dreams.

- Chemist Dmitri Mendeleev apparently woke up one morning with the perfect way to organize the elements in the periodic table.

- René Descartes was a French philosopher and mathematician. He said that a series of vivid dreams helped him create the scientific method — the same method you use for your science projects today.

- Author Robert Louis Stevenson claimed there were "little people" living in his brain who came up with the plot for *The Strange Case of Dr. Jekyll and Mr. Hyde* while he slept.

Could these tales be true? Well, there aren't little people living inside our heads. But our brains do sort our thoughts and strengthen our memories as we snooze.

During the day, we absorb tons of information. We gather input from our senses, we read new things, we learn from our teachers and we practice new sports skills. Every single one of these activities creates connections between the nerve cells in our brains. You might remember from Chapter 1 that these connections are called synapses. We each have billions of them.

But imagine if you remembered everything. Every bad smell you sniffed on the way to school. Every cough you heard in the hallway. Every stray hair of the person in the desk in front of yours. If you stored all that information, your brain might explode. Obviously, you need filters. You need a way to keep what's important and dump what's not.

Scientists believe that sleep serves as our main filter. While we snooze, our brains decide what goes into our mental scrapbook and what goes into the recycling bin.

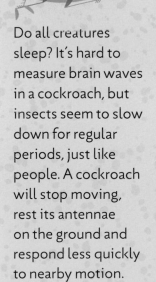

Do all creatures sleep? It's hard to measure brain waves in a cockroach, but insects seem to slow down for regular periods, just like people. A cockroach will stop moving, rest its antennae on the ground and respond less quickly to nearby motion.

Memory Match

When did you learn that the sky is blue? Or that the ocean is wet? How did you learn to use scissors?

You probably don't remember. You might feel as if you've always known these things.

This type of knowledge — common-sense understanding of the world around us — is called semantic memory. It was first described by a pair of Canadian scientists in 1972. More recently, other researchers have discovered that our semantic memories are built and strengthened during sleep.

British neuroscientist Penelope Lewis uses birthday parties to explain how our brains help us develop semantic memories. Imagine you're a toddler at your first birthday party. There are balloons, cake, presents and a swimming pool. A few months later, you go to another friend's birthday party. This time, the party is held at a playground instead of a pool. But there are still balloons, a cake and presents. The third time you go to a birthday party, it's at a gymnasium. Again: balloons, cake and presents.

Penelope believes that as you sleep, your brain compares your new learning to your past experiences. When there's overlap, your brain strengthens those synapses. In this example, there are now strong, repeated connections between birthday parties, balloons, cake and presents.

But the individual parties were all different, for different people, in different places. Those details are probably not as important, and remembering all of them would clutter up your brain. So the connections between random, unconnected details are weakened. Some are entirely swept away.

Dozing Doozies

Every single night, your brain compares, judges and filters. As you drift off to sleep, chemicals and receptors get to work. The synapses responsible for useless information — the fact that your dog farted twice during dinner — are weakened. The synapses for more important information — you love dogs, vets care for dogs and you might want to be a vet when you grow up — are saved and strengthened.

But strangely, sleep can lead us astray. Imagine that your next-door neighbor, Mateo, is invited to every single one of your birthday parties as you grow up. In your mind, birthday parties are linked to balloons, cakes, presents and Mateo.

On your fifth birthday, Mateo stayed home sick. But as you slept that night, your brain stored the memories of your party within the same framework as all your other party memories. By the time a few years have passed, the unconnected details have faded away. You might look back and say, "All my childhood birthday parties were wonderful. And Mateo was at every single one."

You think you remember your fifth birthday clearly. But by storing all birthday party information in the same area, your brain has tricked you. This is called a "false memory," and it's something scientists are only beginning to understand.

The "Aha!" Moment

Insight: a clear, deep and sometimes sudden understanding of a person or thing.

In 2004, German researchers gave three groups of people a complicated test. They showed everyone some strings of numbers. Underneath each string was the beginning of a second list of numbers. It was sort of like a code-breaking puzzle. The participants had to follow specific rules to finish the numbers in each second string.

But there was a secret.

The second string followed a pattern. If people figured out the pattern, they didn't need to remember the rules anymore. They could use the pattern instead. Everything became easier.

So, how many people had this sudden insight? When did they realize the pattern existed?

One group learned the number task in the morning, then stayed awake for the day. A second group did it in the evening, then stayed awake long into the night. A third and final group did their numbers, then tucked themselves into bed for a good night's sleep.

Each group was retested after eight hours. In the awake-all-day group, five out of twenty-two people had figured out the trick. In the awake-all-night group, another five. But in the group that had slept, thirteen out of twenty-two now understood the pattern. That was more than twice as many!

Somehow, immediately going to bed had helped these people gain insight. Like Otto Loewi and his chemical transmitters, or Dmitri Mendeleev and his periodic table, these test participants had figured things out in their sleep.

Scientists know that while we snooze, our brains compare new knowledge to existing memories and sort and file our new learning. While doing that sorting, our brains sometimes find connections. *Hey, this is a pattern!*

And in the morning, we wake to an "aha!" moment of insight and understanding.

Scientists figured this out in 2004, but moms have known for hundreds of years. Just think of this classic mom advice: "Sleep on it. Everything will seem clearer in the morning."

It turns out Mom is right again.

Sleep Soccer

Special offer! Available now! The all-new DOZE-A-MATIC 3000 will help you learn skills in your sleep. You can practice the piano while you snooze, or nap your way to tap-dance success. Get yours while quantities last!

Would you buy that product? Well, don't spend your money just yet. You already have a DOZE-A-MATIC 3000 learning system within your own brain.

UC Berkeley scientist Matthew Walker and his team of researchers have spent years studying how sleep helps us learn motor skills. In one series of experiments, they asked people to learn finger-tapping patterns, sort of like songs on a piano keyboard. The study participants practiced and practiced the patterns, until they couldn't get any better.

Then some of them slept.

Cross-Border Bedtimes

Kids in different countries go to bed at vastly different times. Elementary school students in Hong Kong are wide awake past 10:00 p.m. In Spain, where it's often too hot to play during the afternoon, small children take an afternoon siesta, then swarm the playgrounds late at night. New Zealand and the Netherlands have much earlier bedtimes — little ones are often tucked in by 7:00 or 7:30 p.m. In North America, bedtimes land in the middle, usually between 8:00 and 9:00 p.m. High school students tend to stay up late and sleep in. (Except when they have school!)

How does your clock compare? Do the kids in your class have different routines?

Elite Japanese tennis player Kei Nishikori is also an elite snoozer. He told a CNN reporter that he likes to do two things on his days off: shop and sleep. Swiss player Roger Federer is another sleep star. He tries to get eleven to twelve hours a night!

If people learned their finger-tapping patterns in the morning, then tried them again after a busy day, their performance remained the same. But if people learned in the evening, then had a good night's sleep, they improved — by an average of 20 percent.

Here's what Matthew and his team learned in follow-up studies:

- Doubling your practice time during the day doesn't double your nighttime learning. Somehow, the two learning systems are separate.

- Most sleep-learning happens the night after practice. But a little improvement keeps happening for a few nights afterward.

- Sleep might be particularly helpful with learning rhythm. That could be the rhythm of finger tapping, pedaling a bike or juggling a soccer ball.

There's a lot more to learn about sleep and how it helps us develop motor skills. But even now, professional athletes are paying attention. Many sports teams have hired sleep coaches to help players make the most of daytime and nighttime practice.

Counting Sheep Spindles

To most people, a spindle is a rod used to wind thread or wool. To sleep scientists, it's a sign of learning and intelligence.

When someone wears electrodes as they sleep, researchers see short bursts of brain activity on the EEG machine. These sudden zigzag clusters are called sleep spindles because they're shaped like spools of thread.

Sleep spindles are directly related to learning. If you've studied new math equations all day, you'll probably have more sleep spindles at night. That's your brain transferring information from your thinking centers to your memory centers. People also have more sleep spindles when they're young and learning things constantly, and fewer spindles as they age.

Scientists know that getting a good sleep before a big test or a tough game can help us remember, move and process better. But sleep spindles show that getting a good sleep is just as important the night after an important day of learning.

Sleepy Sniffers

The nose knows ... except when you're sleepy.

American researchers kept a group of volunteers awake for twenty-four hours. Then they asked the volunteers to identify scratch-and-sniff samples of grass, pineapple, pizza and other recognizable smells. Those sleep-deprived sniffers got 84 percent of the smells right. Not too bad. But well-rested sniffers scored 90 percent. If there was a smell-sniffing report card, that would be the difference between a B and an A.

People who are sleep deprived also have more trouble noticing sour tastes, telling the difference between two sounds played at slightly different times and paying attention to things at the edges of their vision.

Supersmart people have more sleep spindles. They're probably genetically programmed that way. Fortunately for the rest of us, even a regular number of spindles gives a boost to our intelligence and memory — every single night.

spindle

Word-Wises

If you ask a group of sleepy people to remember lists of words, they don't do very well. Words such as "butterfly," "bee" or "bird" might fly right out of their brains. But there are exceptions to this rule.

"Poison, death, murder." Those words stick! Why? Scientists think that remembering negative words might help us survive. If you're awake all night after eating poisonous berries, you don't want to eat those berries again in the morning.

The problem isn't with our noses, tongues, ears or eyes. It seems that when we're sleepy, our brains have trouble processing the information from our senses.

The prefrontal cortex is the large area of the brain directly behind your forehead. It does your most complicated thinking. It helps you make decisions, plan your day and express your personality.

When you don't get enough sleep, your prefrontal cortex gets less blood flow. It doesn't burn sugar as effectively. Basically, you can't think as well. You have more trouble paying attention to the small details of the world around you — such as pineapple and pizza scratch-and-sniff.

Shipshape Decisions

Abandon ship!

Your cruise ship's on fire, so you and the other passengers leap into a lifeboat. But there are too many of you. The load is heavy and the boat tilts. As waves rise around you, it looks as if you might sink.

Wait. There's an injured person in your boat. He probably won't survive long anyway. Should you throw him overboard to save yourself and the other passengers?

This type of question is called a moral dilemma. Some dilemmas are easy. (You find a wallet on the playground with $100 inside. Keep it or give it to the principal?) But others, like the lifeboat scenario, mimic life-or-death decisions. And there isn't always a single correct answer.

In daily life, some people are a lot more likely than others to face this sort of question. Firefighters have to decide who to carry first from a burning building. Doctors have to pick which patients to treat most quickly. Soldiers sometimes have only seconds to choose whether or not to shoot someone.

What if the firefighter is tired? What if a soldier has been up all night when she's suddenly faced with a life-altering choice? Does sleep affect ethical decisions?

Scientists in the United States asked a group of soldiers to judge a list of tricky moral situations. They kept the soldiers awake for fifty-three hours, then asked a similar list of questions. When the sleepy soldiers had to figure out emotionally difficult situations, such as whether it was okay to shoot one person to save another, they struggled. They took longer to answer than they would have if they'd slept well. They sometimes chose differently than they had before being sleep deprived.

We now know that lack of sleep affects the prefrontal cortex, where our most important decisions are made. When we're sleep deprived, that area of our brains works more slowly, with less blood flow and less fuel. It's much better to make big decisions when we're well rested. But some people — those soldiers, emergency-room doctors and firefighters —*need* to work night shifts. They *need* to make tough decisions quickly, even when they're tired.

So how can we help them make the best decisions possible? One possible answer: practice. In 2014, a Canadian researcher named Megan Thompson teamed up with a doctor in the Canadian military, Rakesh Jetly. They suggested adding tricky ethical decisions to high-intensity military training exercises. Hopefully, by encountering these situations in training, soldiers will learn to recognize moral dilemmas and be able to respond more quickly.

Chapter 3

Dr. Doze

It's growing dark outside. You click off your bedroom light and snuggle into your pillow. Suddenly, a miniature hospital ward appears in your bedroom. Nurses bustle through to check your blood pressure and heart rate. Doctors assess your insulin levels, your stress hormones and your immune function. Maybe a counselor stops by to chat about your mental health.

That sounds like a lot of activity for an ordinary night!

Well, there are no real nurses, doctors or counselors in your bedroom. But all those checkups really do take place. Every time you drift off to sleep, your brain begins regulating and resetting your body's systems. Your heart function, growth rate, hormones, digestion, insulin levels and more — they're all assessed.

If you've never met your team of invisible health-care practitioners, that's because all of their work takes place while you snooze.

Wacky Wake-a-Thons

In the 1950s, thousands of teens tuned in daily to Peter Tripp's *Your Hits of the Week*. His Top-40 countdown was one of the most popular shows on New York's WMGM radio station.

In 1959, as a publicity stunt and to raise money for charity, Peter pledged to stay awake for 200 hours. He hosted his show from inside a glass box in Times Square.

For the first few days, he was sometimes sleepy. He had trouble regulating his body temperature and he grew a bit glum. But overall, he didn't feel too bad. Then, around day four, things began falling apart. Paranoid and scared, Peter lashed out at the strangers around him. He saw imaginary mice in his box and spiders in his shoes.

What was going on?

The mental and physical symptoms Peter experienced during his wake-a-thon aren't unique. Other people have attempted long periods of wakefulness, with similar results.

In 1965, seventeen-year-old Randy Gardner decided to skip sleep as part of a school science-fair project. After a couple of days, he couldn't concentrate. Simple tongue twisters began to feel complicated. On day four, he thought a lamppost was a person. After nine days, Randy couldn't count backward from one hundred. He was scared and paranoid.

Peter, the radio host, managed to stay awake for 201 hours, then recovered his equilibrium after a restful night. Science-student Randy felt quite normal after a nice deep sleep. He had long-term sleep problems afterward, and no one knows if they stemmed from the marathon or from other stressful events in his life. But 1950s and '60s wake-a-thon experiments helped convince scientists that sleep isn't optional. People can't skip bedtime and expect to function as well as usual.

Still, no one understood *why* sleep is so important or how it affects our bodies at the cellular level. Those are questions that researchers continue to investigate today.

Genetic Junk Removal

Wake-a-thon survivors Peter and Randy went for so long without sleep, their bodies and brains began malfunctioning. If they had stayed awake for even longer, their heartbeats would have become irregular. Eventually, they would have died. People simply can't survive without sleep.

Scientists in Israel may have figured out why. Professor Lior Appelbaum, graduate student David Zada and a team of their fellow scientists studied the nerve cells of young zebra fish. These little swimmers are transparent, so researchers can see right into their brains.

When zebra fish are awake, their neurons are busy communicating. But while the fish sleep, their neurons take a break from regular activities. And they spend the snooze-time repairing damage to their DNA, which is the genetic material inside cells. DNA carries the code that tells each cell what to do and how to do it. Whether we're human or zebra fish, we all need our DNA instructions.

Professor Lior suggests that nerve-cell DNA gets damaged through wear and tear each day, just as a city street might get potholes. During rush hour, the holes grow bigger. But at night, while there are fewer cars, repair crews can patch up the pavement. That leaves everything ready for another day of driving. Or swimming, in the case of zebra fish.

The Night Shift

A good night's sleep really *is* the best medicine. If we sleep well, we're more resistant to colds and flus. We're less likely to get heart disease or cancer. Some research even suggests that vaccinations work better on people who get more rest.

But why? What's happening inside our bodies to boost our immune systems?

Though scientists haven't entirely solved that puzzle, they have some good guesses. It seems that during the day, we have stress hormones running through our bloodstreams. Those hormones keep us alert and attentive. They fight inflammation so our muscles and systems work smoothly.

When we fall deeply asleep, our stress hormones are no longer as active. And that lets immune cells and growth hormones take over. These guys like inflammation. To attack invaders and speed healing, they need a little extra heat and a bit more blood flow to injured areas. So when our stress hormones go off duty for the night, the immune crew gets to work.

It's nice that so much of the immune system's work gets accomplished at night. Having heat and swelling in your system can make you feel unwell. Just as a fever makes you tired and lethargic, a lot of small areas of inflammation can do the same. So why not get it over with while you're snoring?

The immune system has a three-step process:

- It identifies invading germs or toxins.
- It learns how those invaders work, and attacks.
- It stores its new know-how for next time.

Researchers believe sleep is especially vital for the information-storing stage. If we don't snooze for long enough to save our immune-system attack plans, we won't be as well prepared for next time.

Growth Spurts

The human growth hormone (HGH) has a lot of jobs. It prompts cell regrowth. It strengthens bones, increases muscle mass, helps digest sugar and stimulates the immune system. It's the chemical that makes us grow taller in childhood and makes us grow (in other ways) during puberty. And HGH is nocturnal. It's especially active during the first ninety minutes of sleep. When you turn out the lights, it gets growing … and so do you!

All Spaced Out

On board the International Space Station, there are six miniature bedrooms. They feature padded walls with comfy sleeping bags clipped to the edges so sleeping astronauts don't float away. Each astronaut has cozy cotton jammies and an eight-hour assigned sleep time.

For some, it feels strange not to sleep pressed against a mattress. There are often exciting or stressful things for the astronauts to think about, the engines chug and thrum, and the sun rises every ninety minutes as the station orbits the Earth, which can be confusing. But after a week or two on the station, most astronauts say they get used to the changes and start sleeping like rocks ... weightless rocks, that is.

Astronauts need to be in prime mental and physical condition so that they're ready to respond to a crisis. That's why NASA puts a priority on sleep.

Overeating Underwater

Way back in 1948, Nathaniel Kleitman spent two weeks aboard the USS *Dogfish*, an American navy submarine. The crew members usually stood watch for four hours, then had eight hours off. Because they spent part of their eight-hour breaks eating and socializing, they rarely got a full night's rest.

Nathaniel suggested a new schedule that allowed more time for eating and sleeping, but the navy tried it for only eleven days. Why cancel? The officers said their crew members were eating too much!

Nathanial felt the trial was unscientific, and he was unhappy with the results. He suggested that future experiments be run by scientists, not by navy officers.

Other major industries are trying to do the same. On long flights, for example, pilots take turns at the controls. One pilot watches the sky while the other naps. But pilots say they can't sleep well while they're in flight. Any tiny change in the engine noise disturbs them.

Ship engineers say the same thing. And studies have shown that when ship engineers are on call, they don't sleep as well. Even if they're not needed, the knowledge that they *can* be called keeps them semi-alert during the night.

We want our pilots in top condition when they're landing planes, and our ship engineers at their best as they're approaching harbor. So researchers are experimenting with different ways to get these people more rest. One Scandinavian study of more than 500 airline pilots used a cell-phone app to help them track their exercise, sleep and nutrition. It worked! The app prompted the pilots to improve their habits. They found their sleep got better and their fatigue decreased.

For seafarers, another option might be better shift schedules. Many sailors work six hours, then take six hours off. That's a strange way to work and sleep! Slowly, the industry is changing to more standard eight-hour shifts, hoping sailors will get more snoozing.

Ticker Trouble

Imagine you're a doctor. One morning, you see two patients.

- Patient A is overweight. He drinks and smokes too much. He gets very little exercise. But he sleeps eight hours a night.

- Patient B is just as heavy. He also drinks, smokes and doesn't exercise. Plus, he's an insomniac. He's always awake past midnight.

These men are worried about their health. As their doctor, you know they're both at high risk for heart disease. All that eating, drinking and smoking is bad for the ticker. But it's Patient B you need to watch most closely.

Studies show that people who don't sleep well are more likely to develop heart disease, regardless of age and weight or drinking, smoking and exercise habits. People who sleep less than six hours a night die more often from heart attacks. That's partly because sleep helps us digest sugar and fats. It helps us regulate our blood pressure and it gives us a break from our daytime stress hormones.

Our dreamland resets are vitally important. One study found that men with sleep apnea — a disorder that makes people wake up many times per night — have a 58 percent higher rate of heart disease.

The relationship between sleep and cardiovascular disease isn't just a problem for old men. Even teenagers with poor sleep habits are at higher risk of heart issues. Plus, poor sleep contributes to obesity and high blood pressure — problems that can lead to trouble later in life. That's why doctors are paying extra attention to sleep habits these days, for patients young and old and A through Zzzzz.

Snack Attack

If you're a lion, there's really nothing better than a snoozing giraffe. Once a giraffe lies down to sleep, it takes the animal about fifteen seconds to stand up again on its spindly legs. That's plenty of time for a lion to pounce.

So why do giraffes sleep? Wouldn't it be better for them to stay awake and alert, twenty-four hours a day?

Well, they sleep less than we do. They'll often nap while leaning on trees, so they can move quickly if necessary. But like most creatures, giraffes need at least some deep sleep. The only way to get that is to lie down — and risk becoming lunch.

Studying animals such as giraffes has helped convince scientists that sleep is vitally important for health. If it weren't, then evolution would have weeded out the snoozers. The animals that slept more would have been eaten. The animals that slept less would have stayed alive, and their less sleepy offspring would have taken over the world.

None of that happened. The creatures that survived were the ones that slept. Which means the health benefits of sleep must outweigh the risks of becoming a lion's lunch.

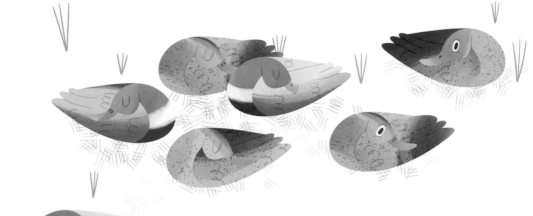

Still, if you're an animal in the wild, it's not always easy or safe to snooze. Some creatures have gone to amazing lengths to protect their dream time.

- In the coral reefs of Australia, parrotfish create pockets of stinky snot around them to turn predators away.

- When dolphins sleep, they shut down only half their brain at a time, switching back and forth every couple of hours.

- Mallard ducks gather in large circles for safety. The ducks inside the circle sleep deeply, while the ducks on the edges sleep with one eye open — literally.

All of these adaptations help creatures get the thing that's most important for their long-term survival: their rest.

When Snoring Gets Scary

Sleep *and* breathe: most of us can do both. For some people, though, it's not so easy. As they drift into deep sleep, the tissues at the back of their throats collapse, blocking the airway. Their oxygen is cut off. After a moment, they jerk awake, breathe, then drift off to sleep again.

In the 1970s, a researcher named Christian Guilleminault read an Italian paper about heavy snorers who developed high blood pressure. He also knew about French research into people who stopped breathing for short periods during the night.

Christian convinced two cardiologists to join his sleep laboratory and monitor snoring patients. They studied about 350 men, women and children with chronic sleep issues. In sixty-two of those patients, the researchers noticed a strange pattern. As the patients drifted into deep sleep, they stopped breathing, woke themselves and fell asleep again. Some people did this hundreds of times. Each time they stopped breathing, their blood pressure spiked. It was as if they were doing intense exercise in their sleep.

Christian and other sleep researchers called this condition sleep apnea. *Apnea* comes from a Greek word meaning "breathless." They learned that the condition is most likely to affect people who are overweight, older or have thick necks or large tonsils. It is more common in smokers and drinkers. But it could occur in skinny people, too, or even in children.

In the 1970s, there weren't many ways to treat sleep apnea. The only real option was a tracheotomy — a permanent hole in the windpipe. It was a solution for only the most severe cases. Doctors struggled to find solutions for the rest of their patients. How could these people get a good night's rest?

Good Night.
Sleep Tight.
Don't Let the Bedbugs Bite.

That bedtime rhyme comes from England. In the 1400s and 1500s, many people slept on straw mats on the floor. But by the 17th century, it was common to own a wooden bed frame with ropes woven across the middle to support the mattress. This kept mice and bugs from getting into the linens. "Sleep tight" meant pull the ropes tight. And "don't let the bedbugs bite" was literal advice!

Joe is an overweight boy who snores loudly and falls asleep during the day. He's a character in *The Pickwick Papers*, written in 1836 by British novelist Charles Dickens. Until Christian Guilleminault began his sleep apnea studies, people who stopped breathing in their sleep were sometimes diagnosed with "Pickwick syndrome."

Wisconsin Wisdom

Imagine what it must feel like to choke and wake up, again and again, all night long. Even if people don't realize it's happening while they sleep, they feel terrible during the day. In the 1980s, American researcher William Dement could see that sleep apnea was a safety concern, too. People who weren't sleeping well were more likely to have car crashes or accidents at work.

He campaigned for more research funding and attention for sleep apnea and related disorders. (Together, these issues are known as sleep disordered breathing, or SDB.) William even presented to the United States Congress in 1986. He convinced the politicians to form a task force to measure the health effects of SDB and the costs of caring for sufferers.

That's when the Wisconsin Sleep Cohort was born. Until then, sleep studies were conducted on small numbers of patients. But researchers at the University of Wisconsin proposed gathering hundreds of patients and studying them for years. They chose the employees of their state. All sorts of people worked for the state government, from lawyers to custodians. The payroll files included young and old, more educated and less educated, rich and relatively poor. It was the perfect group to study.

Eventually, researchers signed up 1500 subjects. One of the first things they learned was that SDB was surprisingly common. About 2 percent of women and 4 percent of men had serious sleep-breathing problems. Less serious problems affected many others.

Since those first findings, the Wisconsin Sleep Cohort has helped researchers produce about one hundred scientific papers about sleep. Every four years, the same participants — the lawyers, custodians, teachers and all

the other state employees who signed up — return to
the lab for assessments of their sleep and health. Today,
more than twenty years after the cohort was formed,
the study continues.

Pressure Players

In 1980, a patient checked into the Royal Prince Alfred
Hospital in Sydney, Australia. He had terrible sleep apnea.
He was waking up every few minutes, all night long.
Dr. Colin Sullivan recommended a tracheotomy, but the
patient refused. He didn't want a hole in his throat.

Colin had one other idea, but he warned the patient that
it was completely experimental.

The patient was desperate. So that same afternoon,
Colin and his staff attached plastic tubes to the patient's
nose. When the patient fell asleep, he began to snore, stop
breathing and wake himself. Colin gradually applied air
pressure through the tubes. And it worked! The constant air
pressure through his nose kept the patient's airway open,
and he was able to breathe regularly.

Colin and his team worked quickly to create and
improve a mask that patients could wear all night.
By 1985, a hundred people were testing the device.
It became known as the CPAP, for continuous
positive airway pressure. And today, millions
of people use it. For patients with sleep apnea,
it improves daytime sleepiness and reduces
the risk of heart disease, cancer, diabetes
and other illnesses.

A 2018 study suggested that almost a
billion people around the world suffer from
sleep apnea, so Colin and other doctors
have many more patients still to reach.

Strange Bedfellows

Did you hear about the newest health fad? It's not a spin class or a low-carb diet. It's called the *get-to-sleep* plan.

Doctors have studied hundreds of thousands of patients in Japan, the United States, Sweden, Australia and Italy. In all their research, they've reached one consistent conclusion: less sleep means a greater chance of weight gain.

Weight gain is only partly explained by lack of exercise or poor eating habits (choosing fatty foods, for example, or eating late at night). For non-sleepers, there's something else going on. And the risks are higher in younger people. Teens who sleep less have a greater chance of gaining weight, and a greater chance of obesity later in life.

Scientists point to a few possible reasons for the sleep-weight connection:

- **Hormones.** When we sleep less, we produce more ghrelin, a hormone that sparks appetite. We produce less leptin, a hormone that makes us feel full.

- **Energy.** When we're sleepy, we burn fewer calories, perhaps because we're too tired to exercise as often or because our body temperatures are lower.

- **Sugar.** With less sleep, our bodies don't use insulin as well: we need more insulin to break down less sugar. Higher insulin levels can cause weight gain and may put us at higher risk of diabetes, too.

Doctors traditionally suggest that patients eat healthy foods and stay active. That seems like reasonable advice. But the least active exercise of all — sleep! — also does a lot to keep us fit.

The Best of Beauty Rest

Researchers in Stockholm, Sweden, showed students photos of well-rested and sleep-deprived people and asked them to rate the pictures for health, attractiveness and tiredness.

They discovered that we humans are really good at noticing the tiny details that show when someone's tired. Though students saw each photo for only six seconds, they could tell which people were sleep deprived. They rated the sleepy people as less healthy and less attractive.

Apparently, the old adage "get your beauty rest" is actually good advice.

Brain Puzzles

"Hey, you!"

"Over here!"

"I need some help!"

What if sleep problems are a way for our brains to signal us? To send a message saying "trouble ahead"? That's what scientists wonder as they explore the links between sleep and mental illness.

Way back in the 1800s, the world's first psychiatrists recognized that poor sleep and mental health issues are linked. But is poor sleep a cause or a symptom? They didn't know. And today's scientists aren't sure either.

Sleep troubles are common in patients with depression, bipolar disorder, schizophrenia, Alzheimer's disease and Parkinson's disease. They can be present at all different stages of the illnesses, in different forms and severities. Some patients experience insomnia; others can't achieve enough deep sleep, when sleep spindles (remember Chapter 2?) are most likely to occur. People with depression often have restless, disordered REM stages.

Finding links between rest and mental illness is complicated because of all the other factors involved — family history, medication use and physical health, for example. One study found that if people had a family history of depression *and* they began dreaming soon after falling asleep, they were more at risk of experiencing depression themselves. But some people dream early in the night and never get depression. Other people experience depression but don't dream early. It's not easy to sort out the causes and effects.

As they work to solve the puzzles of the human brain, researchers hope they can find ways to use sleep problems to help identify people at risk of mental health issues. Then sleep really can act as a neon sign warning "trouble ahead."

By taking sleep issues seriously, doctors might be able to offer early treatment for mental illness, or even — one day — prevention.

Chapter 4

Your Wildest Dreams

What if you told a friend that you were hallucinating last night?

"It was amazing," you'd say. "I fought monsters. I met a rock star. For a while, I even flew through the air."

Your friend might call the doctor!

But that's what we all do, every single night. Though we may not remember in the morning, we spend hours dreaming — imagining things that don't really exist.

So what's with these nightly delusions? Do we really need them?

Some researchers think we're reliving the day's emotions in a safe, sleepy environment. Others think our minds are practicing and preparing for the future.

And what about nightmares? Do they serve a purpose, or do they simply happen when our systems go awry?

From sweet dreams to night terrors, this chapter delves into the strange places between reality and imagination.

Up in Smoke

You may have heard of Sigmund Freud. He's the Austrian doctor who created psychoanalysis in the 1800s. He's famous for:

- reinventing how therapists interact with their patients

- smoking too many cigars

- concocting theories about dreaming

Freud wrote an entire book about our nighttime hallucinations: *The Interpretation of Dreams*, published in 1899. He said there were two parts to every dream. "Manifest content" was the obvious action, which the dreamer could easily understand. "Latent content" was the hidden meaning, which could be discovered through therapy.

He believed that dreams were like codes, and the objects in dreams represented objects or people in real life. He said that when someone had more than one dream in a single night, those dreams had the same meaning, expressed in different ways. And he was convinced that dreams were a way for people to express their deepest wishes — things they might not even realize they wanted.

In the 1800s, as Freud was trying to solve the mysteries of dreaming, there were no scanning machines. There was no way to track or measure what was happening inside the human brain. He could only write down and analyze his own dreams and those of his patients. He was left to guess and wonder about everything else.

That might explain a few of his conclusions.

Freud contributed amazing things to the field of psychoanalysis. But when it came to dreams, he was almost entirely wrong.

Freudian Fun

Here are a few of Freud's dream interpretations. Keep in mind that there's no scientific evidence to support these connections!

If you dream of	It means
houses with smooth walls	men
houses with balconies	women
kings and queens	parents
small animals or rodents	children
water	birth
traveling	death

The REM Connection

Remember Eugene Aserinsky from Chapter 1? He was the guy who discovered the rapid eye movement (REM) stage of sleep in the 1950s. And he quickly learned that when people's eyeballs were moving back and forth under their eyelids, they were likely dreaming.

There was another research superstar interested in dreams in the 1950s. At the medical school in Lyon, France, a young neuroscientist named Michel Jouvet was using an electroencephalogram, or EEG, machine to track the brain waves of cats. Michel then decided to track the neck movements of cats at various times of day and night to see if movement and brain arousal happened at the same time. For this, he used a machine called the electromyogram, or EMG.

While the EEG records the electricity produced by the brain, the EMG records the electricity produced by muscles.

Michel found something unexpected. Sometimes, there was lots of brain stem activity on the EEG, but absolutely no muscle activity in the neck. None! It was as if the cats' neck muscles were occasionally frozen. What was going on?

Michel's work led to an interesting discovery: while we dream, our muscles don't work. There's a good reason for that. In the middle of the night, you might imagine scaling tall buildings, breathing underwater or flying through the air. Obviously, you wouldn't want to try any of those things in real life. By shutting off the areas responsible for movement, our brains keep us safe while we sleep. (The exception: sleepwalking! You'll read more about that later in this chapter.)

Take Your PET to Work

For decades, scientists used fairly simple methods to track sleep. They attached people to EEG and EMG machines. They woke their test subjects again and again to ask whether they were dreaming.

Then, in the 1990s, they began using something called positron emission tomography, or PET. The inventors of PET had found a way to make sugar radioactive. When they gave the sugar to patients, researchers could track the molecules as they traveled through the human body. And since the brain burns sugar as fuel, they could track the molecules right into the brain.

By combining PET with a computerized scan, or CT scan, scientists learned to create 3D images of the brain. For the first time, they could see which areas of the brain were active during the day and during the night.

While people dreamed, the areas of their brains responsible for emotion were working overtime. But the parts responsible for rational thought, organization, self-awareness and memory were barely working at all.

In ancient Egyptian hieroglyphics, dreams were represented by the pictograph of a bed, called a *qed,* combined with an open eye, called a *rwst*. The combination implies that dreamers are awake and asleep at the same time.

Have you ever had a dream that began in your house and ended in a jungle? Or one that involved flying? We're willing to accept strange things in dreams because the areas of our brains responsible for logic aren't awake.

Have you ever dreamed about doing something you would never do in real life? That's also common because the self-awareness part of the brain — the part that helps us make moral choices — gets turned off for the night.

Thanks to PET scans, we also know why it's so hard to remember our dreams. While we're climbing mountains or fighting monsters in REM sleep, our memory centers are taking their own nighttime naps.

Hitting the Pow

You love to ski, and you just had an amazing day shredding the slopes. Then, as you drift off to sleep, you feel yourself moving. It's as if your brain thinks you're still on the mountain!

At first, researchers thought dreams happen only during REM sleep. But by waking people up at various sleep stages and asking them whether or not they were dreaming, scientists slowly learned that dreams also occur just as we're falling asleep, and sometimes when we're in the lighter stages of sleep, too. Some of these early-evening dreams have a lot to do with movement.

In 2007, researchers at the Massachusetts Institute of Technology (MIT) scanned the brain waves of rats as the animals tackled a complicated maze. That night, the rats' brain waves repeated exactly the same patterns. In fact, they repeated the patterns in such detail, the researchers could track the rats' progress through the imaginary maze as the creatures slept.

Harvard researchers put humans through a similar experiment. They sent students through a three-dimensional maze. Half the students then napped for ninety minutes, while the other half relaxed. Who improved when they repeated the task? Only the students who reported dreaming about the maze.

In another Harvard experiment, a researcher named Erin Wamsley asked forty-three college students to ski the virtual slopes of an arcade game called *Alpine Racer II*. After a day of learning, the students donned sleep monitors. Those machines woke them as they drifted off to sleep. Then the students were asked to describe what they were imagining.

Almost half the time, the students were dreaming about skiing.

Did the dreaming brain help the students learn the movements and thought processes required to better play the game? The people who reported thinking about the game as they drifted into dreamland usually performed better the next day.

There's lots more research to be done, but those movement-based dreams as we drift off to sleep may be teaching us more than we know.

Dream Drama

You can't stand a kid in your class, but he's excellent at science. Your teacher just paired the two of you as lab partners. What are you feeling?

- dislike
- jealousy
- ambition
- admiration
- all of the above

You might be angry at your teacher, embarrassed by past events and excited about the science lab, all at the same time.

Life is complicated.

To survive a complex social environment — a classroom, for example — we often need to juggle conflicting emotions while keeping our cool. Not many creatures can do that. When a bear gets angry, it attacks. It doesn't stop to think about its report card first.

Dreams of Love

We know our experiences can change our dreams. It works the opposite way, too! Researchers in New York tracked relationship dreams. They found that when people dreamed of betrayal, they acted more coldly toward their partners the next day. They had more arguments and felt less loving. All this, even though they knew the betrayals were imaginary!

Some researchers believe that dreams might be a key to our human ability to balance our feelings. Dreams give us a safe place to juggle conflicting emotions. You might dream about punching your science partner, for example. That gives you an outlet for your angry thoughts, without getting you suspended from school.

Just as dreaming helps you organize new learning into long-term memories (remember the birthday party and cake connections in Chapter 2?), it also helps organize your feelings. The official term for this is "emotional integration." You sort the day's experiences, match them with past experiences and perhaps adjust your sense of who you are as a person and how you react to the world. That process can help you face other tricky social situations in the future.

Some of us are excitable people who express our emotions openly and loudly. Some of us are quiet, more reflective types. But at night, as we dream … that's when all of us bring the drama.

Much of what scientists understand about dreams and emotion stems from the work of a University of Illinois professor named Rosalind Cartwright. The author of five books and more than 200 scientific papers, she's known as "the Queen of Dreams."

The Trauma Department

In 1989, a huge earthquake rocked the city of San Francisco. It caused about 4000 landslides. A section of the San Francisco–Oakland Bay Bridge collapsed. Sixty-three people died and 3757 were injured.

Emergency responders sprang into action — and so did dream researchers. They recruited students from California and Arizona and asked them to track their dreams in the weeks following the catastrophe.

The students from San Francisco had twice as many nightmares as the students in Arizona. And those who lived closer to the epicenter of the earthquake had more nightmares than those who lived farther away. It was the first time scientists had shown that people incorporate disasters into their dreams, probably as a way to cope with and adjust to stress.

In another study, researchers from Finland traveled to Palestine to study dreams in a war zone. They tracked the dreams of children in the relatively peaceful region of Galilee, as well as the dreams of those in Gaza, where bombs and bullets were a regular occurrence. As the researchers expected, the kids in Gaza had more emotionally intense dreams, often nightmares.

This wasn't necessarily a bad thing. The researchers believed that those scary dreams were perhaps helping kids cope with the frightening things happening in their waking lives.

If you were in a car accident, your dreams afterward might be full of screeching tires, crashing vehicles and blaring sirens. Gradually, as you learn to live with your memories of the accident, your dreams might shift. They might begin to include other scary events from which you escaped, giving you an imaginary happy ending.

Slowly, your dreams might integrate scary things with safe and comforting things.

This sort of dream coping doesn't happen for everyone or in every situation. Sometimes, people who have faced extreme violence experience post-traumatic stress disorder (PTSD). They continue to have stress reactions and disturbing thoughts for months or years after the trauma has ended. Many find themselves stuck with recurrent nightmares. For example, war veterans might go to sleep each night only to relive the heart-pounding fear of the battlefield. It's as if their brains get overwhelmed while trying to process torrents of negative emotion.

Counselors have been able to help some veterans by using a process called "image rehearsal therapy." During the day, veterans reimagine their nightmares but create more hopeful, non-threatening endings. By rehearsing these endings over and over, they help create new ways for their nighttime brains to deal with terrifying events.

Is Your Brain a Crystal Ball?

Can dreams predict the future? There are plenty of stories but absolutely no scientific evidence. Then again, how would you find proof for psychic dreams? As a scientist, you'd need to gather a large group of people and ask them to track their dreams. Then you'd have to wait decades to see if any of those dreams came true. Finally, you'd want to weigh the number of true dreams against the number of false dreams to see if the prophecies happened predictably or by coincidence.

If you were the psychic type, you might predict a massive research headache!

Frankenstein Freak-Outs

It was 1816. Outside a villa in Lake Geneva, Switzerland, a storm raged. Winds howled and branches cracked. Inside, eighteen-year-old Mary woke with a start. She'd dreamed of a monster. A huge, hulking beast put together from the scraps of human bodies.

Two years later, Mary Shelley published *Frankenstein*, one of the world's first horror novels.

Unfortunately, not many of our nightmares turn into creative works of art. So why do we have them? Is a bad dream part of the brain's normal functioning, or is it a glitch in the system? Scientists have no clear answer to that question, but they do have theories. Here are a few of the reasons nightmares might exist:

- **To help us deal with trauma.** From studies like those on the 1989 earthquake survivors or children in war-torn Palestine, we know that bad dreams can help us cope with frightening events.

- **To keep our limbic system running smoothly.** Deep in the center of our brains is the limbic system, sometimes called our "animal brain." It helps process basic emotions such as fear. Perhaps, like every other part of the brain, it needs regular maintenance. And when the cleanup crews move in for the evening, they spark nightmares.

- **To practice for emergencies.** By racing from tidal waves or fighting monsters, our brains might be practicing for real-life fight-or-flight experiences.

In general, children report about one nightmare a month. Adults seem to have fewer. But it's difficult to track the number of bad dreams we experience because we may not remember them in the morning. (If we did, there might be more novels like *Frankenstein*!)

Walking the Walk

In 2000, David Hempleman-Adams became the first human to reach the North Pole in a hot-air balloon. But he almost didn't make it. David was 1280 meters (4200 feet) above the Arctic ice when he drifted off to sleep ... and woke to find himself trying to climb out of the basket! Only his harness saved him.

David was sleepwalking. Or sleep-flying, in his case. About 17 percent of kids and about 5 percent of adults sleepwalk. It's a behavior called a parasomnia, meaning "half-sleep." Part of your brain functions as if you're deeply zonked, and part of it functions as if you're awake.

Night terrors are another type of parasomnia. If you have a night terror, you sit up in bed, gripped by intense fear. Your heart pounds, you gasp for breath and you're often drenched in sweat. Yet after a few minutes, you flop back onto your pillow and forget it ever happened.

Researchers don't know why these nighttime events occur, but there's definitely a genetic link. So if you find yourself walking in your sleep, you can safely blame your parents. If you find yourself high above the Arctic Circle — well, you may have only yourself to blame.

Chapter 5

The Bedtime Blues

Can't sleep? Try a chant, a medicinal plant from Egypt or a round of bloodletting. Okay, maybe not. But those ancient treatments for insomnia prove that sleeplessness is nothing new. And today's fast-paced, technology-rich lifestyle makes it more difficult to unplug than ever before.

An American study called "Monitoring the Future" shows a worrying trend — a trend echoed by other research from around the world. In 1991, about a quarter of American teens were sleep deprived. By 2015, more than 40 percent were sleeping less than seven hours a night. Research recommends 9.25 hours a night for teens; it seems a lot of young people are missing out on sleep.

So why aren't we snoozing, and what can we do about it?

Sleep Sense

You can't sleep! Should you

- watch TV?

- stare at the ceiling?

- count the hours left in the night if you fall asleep at this exact minute?

- ponder global warming?

- decide to sleep in later in the morning?

- nap the next afternoon?

Correct answer: none of the above.

These are all things people do when they can't sleep. And they're all things that sleep doctors say not to do.

Insomnia's a common problem. Studies in North America, Asia and Europe show that about a third of adults have trouble sleeping. An unlucky 10 percent struggle with chronic insomnia. They can't get to sleep or they can't stay asleep. They feel as if they're walking around in a fog all day but unable to rest at night.

Insomnia by itself isn't considered a disease. It's more of a collection of symptoms. Sometimes, it's caused by another disorder: chronic pain, sleep apnea or mental illness. It can also be caused by too much caffeine. Other times, it's the result of stress or anxiety.

Whatever the cause, insomnia rates are high enough to worry doctors and researchers. Sleep-deprived people are more likely to have car accidents, more likely to injure themselves and more likely to make errors at work or school. As we know from Chapter 3, they're also at risk of long-term health problems.

But doctors are beginning to think that some people sleep more than they know. People with insomnia tend to go to bed early, sleep late and nap often. They're always worried about their sleep and constantly trying to "catch up." But what if they're actually sleeping enough already? Research by McGill University professor Henry Olders suggests that many insomniacs get just as much sleep as the rest of us — they just don't realize it.

That may be why a treatment called cognitive-behavioral therapy (CBT) is so effective for sleep problems. Patients learn what behaviors to avoid. (Turn off that TV.) They learn better habits. (Get out of bed at the same time each morning.) And they learn to worry less about the number of hours they're snoozing. It seems that sleep isn't all about the numbers.

Myth Making

Sleep is a tricky thing, even in mythology. The Greek god of sleep was Hypnos, who repeatedly tricked Zeus into dozing off so others could betray him.

Hypnos's mother was the goddess of night, and his father the god of darkness. He married a goddess of relaxation and illusion, and the couple had three sons: one who shape-shifted in human dreams, one who brought nightmares and one who caused hallucinations.

Some of these myths date back 2500 years. Obviously, we modern humans aren't the first to wonder about sleep.

Strange Medicine

Take the wax from the ear of a dog, rub it across your front teeth and fall peacefully asleep. That was advice from Gerolamo Cardano, a mathematician and unlicensed doctor in Italy in the 1500s.

Insomnia treatments in other parts of the world have included a foot lotion made from mouse fat (ancient Rome), eating lettuce (ancient Egypt) and applying live leeches to the skin (America in the 1800s).

Leeches aren't likely to make a comeback anytime soon. But scientists are studying a number of traditional treatments to see if they might be effective. Herbs used to treat sleeplessness in ancient Iran and ancient China seem promising; in scientific trials, some of them worked just as effectively or even more effectively than modern sleeping pills. Doctors in Hong Kong looked at twenty research studies about insomnia and traditional needle acupuncture. They found that, overall, the acupuncture was 16 percent more effective than the most commonly prescribed sleeping pill.

Researchers have turned to Nepal and India for another possibility: meditation. Jason Ong is a professor of neurobiology at the Behavioral Sleep Medicine Lab in Chicago. He assigned insomnia patients to three separate groups. One group simply tracked their sleep. The second group learned mindfulness strategies to reduce stress. The third group practiced mindfulness strategies specifically for insomnia. Both the meditation groups got more sleep than the self-tracking group. The group that learned about mindfulness and insomnia did best of all. Six months after the study began, half of them were sleeping normally, and more than three-quarters had at least improved.

We can't try all the advice from the past. (Poultice of poisonous hemlock? No, thanks.) But there are at least some sleep ideas we might want to revisit.

Gerolamo's earwax cure didn't survive the test of time. But some of his ideas were more successful. You can thank him next time you access your locker, for example — he invented the first combination lock.

Pill Popping

Why not pop a pill to fall asleep? Lots of people do.

About 4 percent of Americans take prescription sleeping pills. 10 percent of Canadians take them, 10 percent of British people and 8 percent of Brazilians. In South Korea, the number of people seeking treatment for sleep disorders went up more than 50 percent between 2000 and 2015. In Norway, the number of teens taking sleeping pills has almost doubled in recent years.

Sleeping pills have changed over the decades. The first popular ones, in the early 1900s, were more like anesthetics. They knocked people right out!

In the 1960s, a different class of drugs arrived. The best known of these is Valium. It eases anxiety, causes muscles to relax and helps people drift off to dreamland. In the 1970s, Valium was the most prescribed drug in America. But it, too, has side effects. It makes people feel drowsy, dizzy or unsteady. In rare cases, the drug causes mood changes, confusion or hallucinations.

Today, people can choose between a variety of sleep aids. There are antihistamines, which are available without a prescription. There are different forms of melatonin, which are supposed to help people sleep more naturally. And there are stronger medications such as zaleplon and zolpidem, nicknamed "Z-drugs." These work a lot like Valium but have fewer side effects.

Even though today's sleeping pills are safer than the ones of forty years ago, they still have downsides.

Some are addictive. Some can cause headaches, memory loss or dizziness. In some cases, overdosing on the pills can be fatal. And even when they're taken correctly, medications don't always help people achieve the deep sleep their bodies need.

So if you're struggling with sleep, talk to your parents and your doctor. Consider all your options. And read on to discover some of the other ways people achieve their dreams — literally.

Hunting and Gathering Data

How did people sleep before televisions, car horns and sirens? To answer that question, scientists from New Mexico and California traveled around the world. They studied sleep habits in three groups of people who live traditionally, without electricity, hunting for and gathering their food:

- the Hadza people in northern Tanzania

- the Ju/'hoansi-San people in Namibia

- the Tsimane people in Bolivia

None of these groups use lights or machines. They have no TVs, electric fans, bedside lamps or smartphones.

The sleep habits of all three groups were remarkably similar. People fell asleep about three hours after sunset and woke a little before sunrise. They slept a bit more in winter and a bit less in summer. On average, they slept between 6.9 and 8.5 hours per night. They didn't wake often at night, and they didn't nap often during the day — although there were a few snoozes on hot summer afternoons.

Hardly anyone had trouble sleeping. In fact, when researchers wanted to ask about insomnia, they first had to explain what it was. There is no translation for the word in the Hadza, San or Tsimane languages.

"I am so inflicted with the insomnia of this eternal night, that I rise at any time between midnight and noon." Elisha Kent Kane, an American medical officer and explorer, wrote those frustrated words in his journal while traveling the Arctic in 1856.

Power Nap

Artist Salvador Dali was known for his wild creativity. He was born in Spain in 1904 and began exhibiting his paintings when he was only fourteen. He became famous for surrealism — he combined strange symbols, colors and shapes into fantastical paintings and sculptures.

Salvador had a unique way of unleashing his creativity. He called it "the slumber with a key."

1. Place a dinner plate on the floor beneath the left arm of your chair.

2. Sit in the chair with your head tilted back.

3. Hold a key lightly between the thumb and forefinger of your left hand.

4. Dangle your left hand over the arm of your chair, above the plate.

5. Doze off.

As soon as Salvador fell asleep in this position, the key would slip from his fingertips and clatter onto the plate, waking him. His "nap" was less than a second long. But the artist felt that this was enough to reawaken the creative urges within him.

Science says he might be right. Salvador loved to paint from dreams. Today, we know that some of our first dreams occur in the moments immediately after we drift off to sleep.

Though not many people try to nap for milliseconds, there have been plenty of committed nappers in history, from French emperor Napoleon Bonaparte to American inventor Thomas Edison. So what does science have to say about the traditional "power nap"?

Researchers believe that a twenty-minute doze in the afternoon can help you feel more alert. Longer naps might help you remember things or make you feel more creative, but they can also mess with your nighttime sleep. The official advice seems to be: catnap with caution.

Blind Mice (More Than Three)

We all know we're not supposed to use phones and tablets before bed. But why?

Well, it started with some blind mice.

Way back in the 1920s, an American researcher named Clyde E. Keeler accidentally bred some mice without rods or cones in their eyes. You might remember learning about rods and cones in science class. They're the cells in our retinas that allow us to see. Rods give us sight in dim light. Cones give us color vision.

Without rods or cones, Clyde's mice were blind. But Clyde noticed something strange — the animals' pupils still responded to light. Even without their vision cells, the mice were somehow detecting light.

Seventy years later, other scientists discovered that blind mice, without rods or cones, still had circadian rhythms. They still produced melatonin. There was something unexplained going on.

Finally, in 2002, Professor David Berson and his team at Brown University discovered a new type of light-sensitive cell. They had tracked, measured and tested for years and eventually detected a specific kind of cell that they thought was receiving light signals. They placed one under a microscope, hooked it to a machine that tracks electricity and exposed the cell to light.

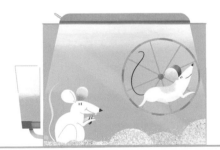

Nothing happened.

Everyone's shoulders slumped.

Then, suddenly, a blip from the electricity machine.

The cell had registered the light! It simply worked more slowly than rods and cones.

David and his team had discovered photosensitive (light-sensitive) ganglion cells.

Ganglion cells are neurons on the inner layer of the retina. They're responsible for taking the information from our rods and cones and transferring it, through their long "tails," to the brain. It turns out that about two out of every thousand ganglion cells in our retinas have a superpower: a special pigment that allows them to sense light.

Now that scientists understand that some of our ganglion cells are light sensitive, they know that our circadian systems are getting special signals. Sometimes, even people who are visually impaired — people whose rods and cones aren't working properly — can still receive light/dark messages from these special cells.

There's one other interesting thing about light-sensitive ganglion cells. They're especially attuned to blue light. That's the kind of light emitted by things such as LED bulbs, cell phones and tablets.

Imagine you're hanging out in your living room with the LED lamp on. You're watching TV, sending the occasional text and waiting to get sleepy. Your conscious mind thinks it's almost bedtime. But you're absorbing blue light from three different sources — the lamp, the TV and your phone. So your light-sensitive ganglion cells are telling your brain it's daytime. Talk about mixed messages!

Blue Light Balance

Night-shift workers constantly fight their own circadian rhythms, trying to stay awake through the dark hours of the early morning. Under those conditions, the brain doesn't work as quickly. For workers in Iran's oil refineries, that's a major problem. A midnight mix-up in the control room could result in disaster.

To help workers stay awake on the job, scientists tried blue light. After seven shifts under new, super-powered bulbs, workers took tests to measure their memory and multi-tasking skills. They passed with flying colors. The blue light had tricked their brains into thinking night was day.

Pump It Up

Exercise and sleep are like conjoined twins — they share all sorts of our body systems. Both affect our hormones, our immune systems, our moods and our brain waves. Great sleeps can improve our motor skills and concentration. In the same way, great workouts can improve our slumber.

Here are a few ways you can help your bod and bedtime all at once.

- **Exercise often.** Regular exercise increases both total sleep time and the amount of deep sleep. One study followed fifty-one teens for three weeks. When they exercised for thirty minutes a day, their sleep improved, along with their moods and concentration abilities.

- **Exercise whenever.** Doctors used to say we shouldn't exercise in the evening, but recent research suggests that's not true. It doesn't matter when you exercise, as long as you're not sacrificing sleep time to get your sweat on.

- **Exercise your endorphins.** Those are the hormones that help your body handle pain. A burst of them after exercise is sometimes called a "runner's high." Physical activity together with increased endorphins has been shown to improve people's moods and decrease anxiety. Less stress makes it easier to drift into dreamland.

Scientists still have tons of questions about the ways sleep and exercise relate. Both affect heart rate and body temperature. But how do our bodies adjust? How does that relationship work in seniors? What about kids?

It might take a few more years on the research treadmill to chase down all the answers.

The Chocolate Choice

Would you like an iced tea? A cold soda? Or a tasty chocolate bar?

Those seem like innocent questions, but caffeine — found in tea, chocolate and most colas — is a major sleep-killer. Throughout the day, a chemical called adenosine accumulates in our bodies. It's part of the sleep pressure system explained by Alexander Borbély in Chapter 1. The adenosine is supposed to send sleepy-sounding messages to special receptors in our brains.

Then caffeine swoops in, wearing an adenosine disguise. It blocks the receptors, so our sleep-pressure chemicals can't get through. For a while, we feel extra energetic. Then, when the caffeine wears off, we might feel extra tired.

One study in Australia found that 87 percent of eight- to twelve-year-old kids consumed caffeine in chocolate bars, coffee, tea or colas. The more caffeine they ate or drank, the more likely the kids were to have problems with sleep, morning tiredness and anxiety. A study of thirteen-year-olds in Portugal found similar results: more caffeine equaled less sleep.

The Portuguese study found another thing that matched American research: kids who consume more caffeine also spend more time on screens. It's not clear whether screen use prompts extra drinking and snacking, or caffeine use keeps kids awake longer to use their screens. But since we know that both screens and caffeine are bad for sleep, a combination of the two is the perfect recipe for nighttime trouble.

Still can't sleep? Call the sandman. He's a mythical figure from Western and Northern Europe who sprinkles magical sand into people's eyes and helps them drift away for the night.

Sleepless in Seattle

Go to bed at the same time each night and wake up at the same time every morning. That's a common piece of sleep advice. There's just one tiny problem. Your favorite wake-up time might be 10:00 a.m. And school starts at 8:00 a.m.

Remember Mary Carskadon from Chapter 1? She's the sleep scientist who invites kids to camp each summer and studies their brain waves. She helped develop the idea that teens experience "phase delay." Their bodies produce melatonin later at night, so they don't fall asleep until well after dark. Then they need to catch up in the morning.

Mary quickly convinced her fellow scientists. But it's taken her a lot longer to convince high school principals — especially in the United States, where school usually starts early.

Principals thought it sounded like a massive headache. Changing start times would involve rerouting the school buses and rescheduling after-school activities. Some parents would have to pick up their little kids an hour earlier than their big kids. It just wasn't practical. Besides, give the kids an extra hour in the mornings and they might just stay up an hour later each night!

But slowly, Mary and other sleep scientists have convinced more and more schools to try. In 2016, the University of Washington teamed up with the Seattle School Board to test the relationship between school start times and sleep. In the fall of 2016, researchers gave wristwatch trackers to sophomore students at two local high schools. For two weeks, the students wore the watches, kept sleep diaries, tracked their daytime sleepiness and filled out questionnaires.

In the spring, the district shifted high school start times by almost an hour so students could sleep a little longer in the mornings. Again, the sophomores donned their wristwatches and got out their sleep diaries.

The results were clear. In the spring, students got an average of thirty-four extra minutes of sleep each night. They earned better grades. They felt less sleepy in class. Both attendance and punctuality improved. And what about the worry that students would stay up extra late? According to the tracking watches, it never happened.

Other school boards around the world are shifting. When the Keewatin–Patricia District School Board in northern Ontario shifted start times to 9:00 a.m., attendance increased and drop-out rates decreased. Alice Miller School outside Melbourne, Australia, has gone one step further — their classes don't start until 10:00 a.m.!

In the United States, most middle schools and high schools still start at or before 8:30 a.m. But as doctors, parents and teens demand changes, more and more schools are making phase delays of their own.

The Snooze Button

There's still a lot to learn about our bodies, our brains and our sleeping patterns. But doctors and scientists do agree on a few pieces of sleep advice.

- Put away your electronics.
- Cut the caffeine.
- Get some exercise.
- Go outside in the sunshine.
- Meditate.

- Keep your bedroom nice and cool, quiet and dark.
- Dim the lights in your house an hour or two before bed.
- Go to bed at the same time each night.
- Wake up at the same time, too. (Even on weekends!)

If none of that works, it's time to see your doctor.

Sleep Frontiers

Could passengers one day fly to Mars in a sort of stasis state? That sounds like a science-fiction scenario, and it is — for now. But NASA recently funded research for something it calls "torpor-inducing Mars transfer habitats." Basically, scientists want to slow astronauts' bodies into a state of hibernation. If they succeed, travelers could survive for months with less need for food and oxygen. Their bodies might be better able to handle zero gravity and higher radiation levels.

With projects like this one, sleep research is zooming toward the far reaches of the solar system. Meanwhile, other advancements are going tiny — microscopically tiny. As scientists explore the ways our neurons communicate, they discover more and more connections between our sleeping and awake selves. Our slumbers affect our emotions, our memories and our physical coordination. And our daytime exercise, meals and learning affect our sleep.

We often think of sleeping and waking as opposites, like night and day or darkness and light. But with each new research project, scientists learn that our consciousness has its own cycles and systems, intricately connected to one another. Our brains and our bodies don't shut down for the night. They continue growing and learning in ways we don't completely understand.

Just as space has yet to be fully explored, there are plenty of new frontiers inside the human brain.

More to Explore

Patterson, Lindsay, and Marshall Escamilla. "The Sleep Camp Experiment." *Tumble Science Podcast for Kids*. Podcast audio, May 18, 2018. http://app.kidslisten.org/ep/Tumble-Science-Podcast-for-Kids-The-Sleep-Camp-Experiment.

Start School Later. Website. https://www.startschoollater.net.

Suni, Eric. "Teens and Sleep." Reviewed by Alex Dimitriu. SleepFoundation.org (OneCare Media). Last modified August 5, 2020. https://www.sleepfoundation.org/articles/teens-and-sleep.

Vedantam, Shankar. "Radio Replay: Eyes Wide Open" *Hidden Brain*. Podcast audio, September 21, 2018. https://www.npr.org/2018/09/20/650114225/radio-replay-eyes-wide-open.

Vo, Dzung X. *The Mindful Teen: Powerful Skills to Help You Handle Stress One Moment at a Time*. Oakland, CA: Instant Help, 2015.

Selected Sources

Chapter 1

Carskadon, Mary A. "Sleep in Adolescents: The Perfect Storm." *Pediatric Clinics of North America* 58, no. 3 (June 2011): 637–647.

Crowley, Stephanie J., Christine Acebo, and Mary A. Carskadon. "Sleep, Circadian Rhythms, and Delayed Phase in Adolescence." *Sleep Medicine* 8, no. 6 (September 2007): 602–612.

Kaplan, Robert M. "The Mind Reader: The Forgotten Life of Hans Berger, Discoverer of the EEG." *Australasian* 19, no. 2 (April 2011): 168–169.

Kleitman, Nathaniel, and Hortense Kleitman. "The Sleep–Wakefulness Pattern in the Arctic." *The Scientific Monthly* 76, no. 6 (June 1953): 349–356.

Mendelson, Wallace B. *The Science of Sleep: What It Is, How It Works, and Why It Matters*. Chicago: University of Chicago Press, 2017.

Millett, David. "Hans Berger: From Psychic Energy to the EEG." *Perspectives in Biology and Medicine* 44, no. 4 (Autumn 2001): 522–542.

Sannita, Walter G. "Higher Brain Function and the Laws of Thermodynamics: Hans Berger and His Time." *Journal of Psychophysiology* 31, no. 1 (2007): 1–5.

Schenck, Carlos H. *Sleep: The Mysteries, the Problems, and the Solutions*. New York: Avery, 2007.

Zisapel, Nava. "New Perspectives on the Role of Melatonin in Human Sleep, Circadian Rhythms and Their Regulation." *British Journal of Pharmacology* 175, no. 16: 3190–3199.

Chapter 2

Barnes, Christopher M., et al. "Sleep and Moral Awareness." *Journal of Sleep Research* 24, no. 2 (April 2015): 181–188.

Killgore, William D. S., and Sharon A. McBride. "Odor Identification Accuracy Declines Following 24 h of Sleep Deprivation." *Journal of Sleep Research* 15, no. 2 (June 2006): 111–116.

Lewis, Penelope A. *The Secret World of Sleep: The Surprising Science of the Mind at Rest*. New York: Palgrave MacMillan, 2013.

Lewis, Penelope A., and Simon J. Durrant. "Overlapping Memory Replay During Sleep Builds Cognitive Schemata." *Trends in Cognitive Sciences* 15, no. 8 (August 2011): 343–351.

Lockley, Steven W., and Russell G. Foster. *Sleep: A Very Short Introduction*. Oxford: Oxford University Press, 2012.

Mindell, Jodi A., et al. "Cross-Cultural Differences in Infant and Toddler Sleep." *Sleep Medicine* 11, no. 3 (March 2010): 274–280.

Thompson, Megan M., and Rakesh Jetly. "Battlefield Ethics Training: Integrating Ethical Scenarios in High-Intensity Military Field Exercises." *European Journal of Psychotraumatology* 5, no. 1 (August 2014): 23668.

Wagner, Ullrich, et al. "Sleep Inspires Insight." *Nature* 427 (January 2004): 352–355.

Walker, Matthew P., et al. "Sleep and the Time Course of Motor Skill Learning." *Learning & Memory* 10, no. 4 (July 2003): 275–284.

Zada, D., et al. "Sleep Increases Chromosome Dynamics to Enable Reduction of Accumulating DNA Damage in Single Neurons." *Nature Communications* 10 (March 2019): 895. 1–12.

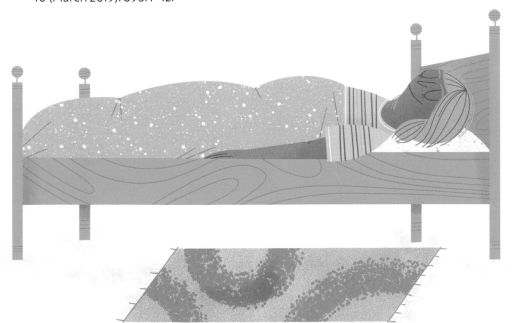

Chapter 3

Ahlheim, Hannah. "Governing the World of Wakefulness: The Exploration of Alertness, Performance, and Brain Activity with the Help of 'Stay-Awake Men' (1884–1964)." *Anthropology of Consciousness* 24, no. 2 (September 2013): 117–136.

Bartlett, Thomas. "The Stay-Awake Men." *The New York Times,* April 22, 2010.

Beccuti, Guglielmo, and Silvana Pannain. "Sleep and Obesity." *Current Opinion in Clinical Nutrition and Metabolic Care* 14, no. 4 (July 2011): 402–412.

Besedovsky, Luciana, Tanja Lange, and Jan Born. "Sleep and Immune Function." *European Journal of Physiology* 463 (January 2012): 121–137.

Cappuccio, Francesco P., and Michelle A. Miller. "Sleep and Cardio-Metabolic Disease." *Current Cardiology Reports* 19, no. 11 (September 2017): 110.

Guilleminault, C., A. Tilkian, and W. C. Dement. "The Sleep Apnea Syndromes." *Annual Review of Medicine* 27 (February 1976): 465–484.

Lewis, Penelope A. *The Secret World of Sleep.* New York: Palgrave MacMillan, 2013.

Lockley, Steven W. and Russell G. Foster. *Sleep: The Surprising Science of the Mind at Rest.* Oxford: Oxford University Press, 2012.

McGirr, Michael. *Snooze: The Lost Art of Sleep.* New York: Pegasus Books, 2017.

Van Drongelen, Alwin, et al. "Evaluation of an mHealth Intervention Aiming to Improve Health-Related Behavior and Sleep and Reduce Fatigue Among Airline Pilots." *Scandinavian Journal of Work, Environment, and Health* 40, no. 6 (August 2014): 557–568.

Young, Terry. "Rationale, Design and Findings from the Wisconsin Sleep Cohort Study: Toward Understanding the Total Societal Burden of Sleep Disordered Breathing." *Sleep Medicine Clinics* 4, no. 1 (March 2009): 37–46.

Chapter 4

Arnulf, Isabelle, Colette Buda, and Jean-Pierre Sastre. "Michel Jouvet: An Explorer of Dreams and a Great Storyteller." *Sleep Medicine* 49 (September 2018): 4–9.

Grenell, Gary. "Affect Integration in Dreams and Dreaming." *Journal of the American Psychoanalytic Association,* 56, no. 1 (March 2008): pp. 223–251.

Helminen, Elisa, and Raija-Leena Punamäki. "Contextualized Emotional Images in Children's Dreams: Psychological Adjustment in Conditions of Military Trauma." *International Journal of Behavioral Development* 32, no. 3 (May 2008): 177–187.

Hobson, J. Allan. *Dreaming: An Introduction to the Science of Sleep.* Oxford: Oxford University Press, 2002.

Levin, Ross, and Tore Nielsen. "Nightmares, Bad Dreams, and Emotional Dysregulation: A Review and New Neurocognitive Model of Dreaming." *Current Directions in Psychological Science* 18, no. 2 (April 2009): 84–88.

Luppi, Pierre-Hervé. "Obituary: Michel Jouvet (1925–2017), The Father of Paradoxical Sleep." *Journal of Sleep Research* 26, no. 6 (November 2017): 832–834.

Sejnowski, Terrence. "How are Memories Consolidated During Sleep and Why Do We Dream?" *Biological Psychiatry* 81 no. 10, Supplement: 72nd Annual Scientific Convention and Meeting (May 15, 2017): S1.

Stickgold, Robert. "Sleep-Dependent Memory Consolidation." *Nature* 437 (October 2005): 1272–1278.

Wamsley, Erin J., et al. "Cognitive Replay of Visuomotor Learning at Sleep Onset: Temporal Dynamics and Relationship to Task Performance." *Sleep* 33, no. 1 (January 2010): 59–68.

Chapter 5

Andalib, Sasan, et al. "Sedative and Hypnotic Effects of Iranian Traditional Medicinal Herbs Used for Treatment of Insomnia." *EXCLI Journal* 10 (2011): 192–197.

Chennaoui, Mounir, et al. "Sleep and Exercise: A Reciprocal Issue?" *Sleep Medicine Reviews* 20 (April 2015): 59–72.

Dunster, Gideon P., et al. "Sleepmore in Seattle: Later School Start Times Are Associated with More Sleep and Better Performance in High School Students." *Science Advances* 4, no. 12 (December 2018): eaau6200.

Motamedzadeh, Majid, et al. "The Effect of Blue-Enriched White Light on Cognitive Performances and Sleepiness of Night-Shift Workers: A Field Study." *Physiology and Behavior* 177 (August 2017): 208–214.

Münch, Mirjam, and Aki Kawasaki. "Intrinsically Photosensitive Retinal Ganglion Cells: Classification, Function and Clinical Implications." *Current Opinion in Neurology* 26, no. 1 (February 2013): 45–51.

Ong, Jason C., et al. "A Randomized Controlled Trial of Mindfulness Meditation for Chronic Insomnia." *Sleep* 37, no. 9 (September 2014): 1553–1563.

Scult, Matthew. "The Eyes Have It: Getting to Know Professor David Berson." *Biomed Newsphage* (blog), Brown University, May 14, 2009. https://blogs.brown.edu/behind-the-science/2009/05/14/the-eyes-have-it-getting-to-know-professor-david-berson. Accessed January 29, 2019.

Singh, Amrinder, and Kaicun Zhao. "Treatment of Insomnia with Traditional Chinese Herbal Medicine." *International Review of Neurobiology* 135 (2017): 97–115.

Twenge, Jean M., et al. "Decreases in Self-Reported Sleep Duration Among U.S. Adolescents 2009–2015 and Association with New Media Screen Time." *Sleep Medicine* 39 (November 2017): 47–53.

Watson, Emily J., et al. "The Relationship between Caffeine, Sleep, and Behavior in Children." *Journal of Clinical Sleep Medicine* 13, no. 4 (April 2017): 533–543.

Yetish, Gandhi, et al. "Natural Sleep and Its Seasonal Variations in Three Pre-Industrial Societies." *Current Biology* 25, no. 21 (November 2015): 2862–2868.

Yeung, Wing-Fai, et al. "Traditional Needle Acupuncture Treatment for Insomnia. A Systemic Review of Randomized Controlled Trials." *Sleep Medicine* 10, no. 7 (August 2009): 694–704.

Index